Signing

BLACKLINE MASTERS

GRADES 3-6

SHARE the Music

McGRAW-HILL

SERIES AUTHORS

Judy Bond
Coordinating Author

Rene Boyer-Alexander

Margaret Campbelle-Holman

Marilyn Copeland Davidson
Coordinating Author

Robert de Frece

Mary Goetze
Coordinating Author

Doug Goodkin

Betsy M. Henderson

Michael Jothen

Carol King

Vincent P. Lawrence
Coordinating Author

Nancy L. T. Miller

Ivy Rawlins

Susan Snyder
Coordinating Author

Contributing Writer
Janet McMillion

McGraw-Hill
School Division
New York   Farmington

Teri Burdette, the writer of the two *Signing* books for ***Share the Music***, is a music teacher at Lucy Barnsley Elementary School in Rockville, Maryland. Since 1980 she has taught deaf, hearing impaired, and hearing students in a mainstreamed program. Teri formed the Flying Fingers, a group of performing fifth graders, to help raise the awareness that "Music and Sign Language Are for Everyone!"

McGraw-Hill School Division

A Division of The McGraw-Hill Companies

Copyright © McGraw-Hill School Division

All rights reserved. Permission granted to reproduce for use with McGraw-Hill SHARE THE MUSIC.

McGraw-Hill School Division
Two Penn Plaza
New York, NY 10121

Printed in the United States of America

ISBN 0-02-295432-5/ 3-6

5 6 7 8 9 024 04 03 02

INTRODUCTION

In the music classroom, sign language becomes more than a mode of communication. It offers yet another unique vehicle for learning and musical expression. Sign language can enhance the performance of a song and, as in choral choreography, add interest for the participant as well as the observer.

The use of sign language in songs is conceptual, not literal. The objective is to paint a picture, and it is therefore not necessary to sign every word, although all words are sung. Articles and many pronouns are eliminated in sign. Also, since a word may have more than one meaning, it may have more than one sign.

In conversation many words do not have specific signs and are fingerspelled using the manual alphabet. Fingerspelling is so small it is usually avoided in songs. However, since many signs are based on the manual alphabet, it is included at the back of the book as a reference guide. If a particular phrase or idea does not lend itself to sign, a combination sign, gesture, and mime is used. Examples of this are indicated by the use of the word *Gesture* at the beginning of the signing directions in this book.

Sign language does not rely solely on the use of hands. Facial expressions and body movements are very important; this is how the mood of the song is conveyed to the audience.

Signs should flow from one to the next, keeping in mind the rhythm of the song, and should match the length of the phrases. The signing of songs should also include very large movements so that the audience can see them.

The illustrations and signing instructions in this book are directed to a right-handed student. Students who are left-handed should reverse the hands. However, for beginning sign-language work, don't worry about right and left. If students ask which hand to use, respond by saying, "The hand that you write with is the one that does the most moving."

When students perform, put the left-handed signers on the ends of the rows to avoid collision with fellow students. For best visual results, have students wear colors contrasting to skin color so that the hands are highlighted. Solid shirts are a must since prints and geometrics confuse the eye.

There are many different ways to sign the same phrase or thought. The sign language in this book is *one* approach to learning songs in sign. Also, sign language is colloquial and can vary in different parts of the country.

Students should start with vocabulary that is meaningful. It is fine to sign just a few appropriate words or to use a sign ostinato. Using a "how to" verbiage while showing students a sign can help those who learn by hearing, as watching can help those who learn better by seeing. Don't worry about perfection. The emphasis should be on enjoyment and fun! The signers' hands will become better able to find the positions with each new experience.

—Teri Burdette

TABLE OF CONTENTS

		TEACHER'S EDITION page	SIGNING MASTER page

GRADE 3

GRADE 3

Jambo (Hello)

1. hello

(Gesture) Wave your raised right hand, palm facing front and fingers open, from side to side.

2. ev'rybody

(Gesture) Hold your hands together, with palms up and fingers touching. Then move them apart in a sweeping gesture.

McGraw-Hill

Turn the Glasses Over

1. sailing

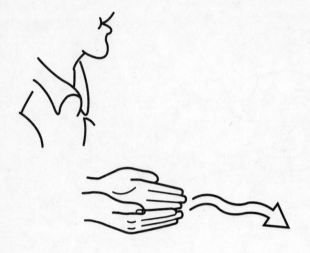

Form a boat with your hands, little fingers touching, and move it forward.

2. east

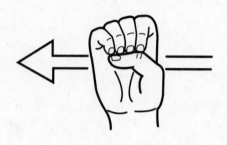

Move your right hand, in the "E" position, to the right.

3. west

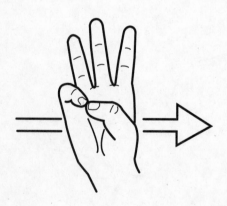

Move your right hand, in the "W" position, to the left.

4. ocean

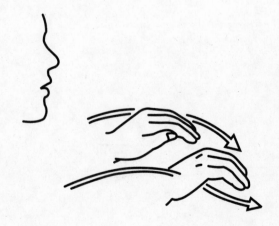

Move your hands forward, making the motion of waves.

Name_____

1. now

Hold both hands in the "Y" position, palms up. Then drop them down. (Use this only the first time it is sung.)

2. let

With palms facing each other and fingers pointing away from your body, move your hands in a scooping motion—down, then up.

3. fly

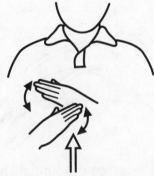

Raise your open hands, palms down and right index finger against left little finger, while moving the fingers up and down.

4. way up high

Using the sign for *fly*, move your hands way up high.

5. way

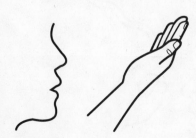

Gesture upward with your open right hand, palm facing in.

6. middle

Move your bent right hand in a circle, then down into your left palm. Make the sign up high, close to the gesture for *way*.

7. air (sky)

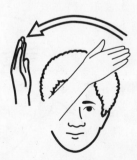

Make a large arc above your head with your right hand.

SIGNING MASTER S•3•4

We're Off to See the Wizard

1. follow

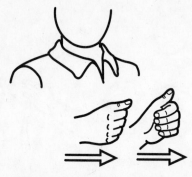

Hold both of your hands in the "A" position, with the right hand behind the left. Then move the hands forward.

2. yellow

Shake your right hand, in the "Y" position, while turning it back and forth at the wrist. (Add this sign only after you have mastered the rest.)

3. road

Hold your open hands facing each other, fingers pointing forward and thumbs up, and move them forward in a winding manner.

4. rainbow

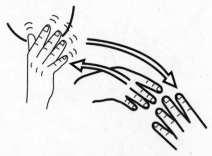

Wiggle the fingertips of your right hand on your chin. Then, with hands in the "4" position, move the right hand to touch fingertips with the left and away in an arc.

5. fellow (boy)

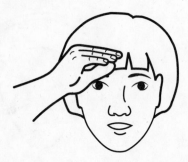

Hold your right hand, palm down, at your forehead, and open and close it once or twice.

6. dream

Wiggle your right index finger as you move it away from your forehead.

McGraw-Hill

Name _____

1. ev'ry

With both hands in the "A" position, draw your right thumb down your left thumb several times.

2. night

Rest your right hand, in a bent position, on top of your left hand, which is held palm down.

3. when

Move your right index finger around your left index finger, held palm in, and end with the tips of the two fingers touching.

4. sun goes in (sunset)

Hold your left arm parallel to the ground. Move your right hand, in the "O" position, down behind the left arm.

5. hang down my head (discouraged)

Bend your head forward, and move the middle finger of each hand down your body.

6. mournful (sad)

Move both hands, palms in and fingers separated, down in front of your face, and show sadness in your face and body.

7. cry

Trace tears from your eyes down your face with your index fingers.

McGraw-Hill

I Got a Letter

1. got (accept)

Begin with hands open and fingers spread. Move the hands to your chest, closing the fingertips of each hand as they move.

2. letter

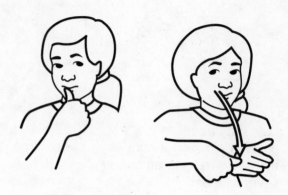

Touch your right thumb to your tongue. Then move the thumb down into your left palm to show stamping a letter.

3. morning

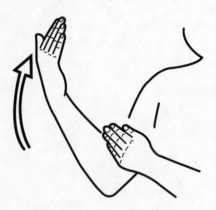

Place the fingertips of your left hand in the bend of your right arm. Then move your open right palm upward toward your body.

4. yes

Move your right hand, in the "S" position, up and down to show a head nodding. Sign one slow nod for *oh* and one for *yes*.

McGraw-Hill

Name_____

---

1. good

Touch your lips with the fingertips of your right hand. Then move the hand into the open palm of your left hand.

---

2. news (inform)

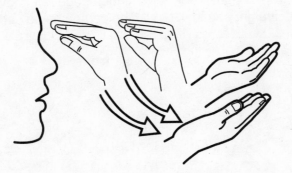

Hold both of your hands in a flat "O" position at your forehead. Then move the hands forward and outward while opening them, with palms up. (This is to show taking knowledge from the head and giving it away.)

Use with pages 260, 281. • Grade 3

McGraw-Hill

This Land Is Your Land (Page 1)

1. this

(Gesture) Hold your hands together, with palms up and fingers touching. Then move them apart in a sweeping gesture.

2. land

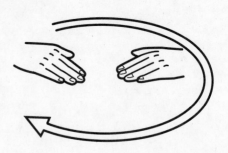

(Gesture) With both palms down and hands open, make a large circle with your right hand over your left hand.

3. is

Touch your lips with the tip of your right index finger. Then move the hand straight ahead.

4. your

Hold your right hand with palm out and fingers together. Move the hand out toward the person being spoken to.

5. my

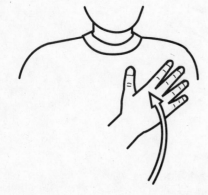

Touch your chest with your open right hand.

6. from

Point your left index finger up. Touch your right hand, in the "X" position, to the left index finger. Then move the right hand away.

8

McGraw-Hill

Name_____

This Land Is Your Land (Page 2)

7. California 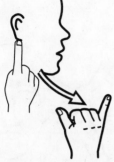 Touch your earlobe with the index finger of your right hand. Then move the hand down and into the "Y" position.	**8. to**  Point the index finger of your right hand to the tip of the upright index finger of your left hand.
9. New York 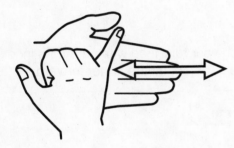 Move your right hand, in the "Y" position, back and forth in the open palm of your left hand.	**10. island** 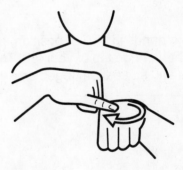 Make a circle with your right hand, in the "I" position, on the back of your left closed fist.
11. redwood forest (forest) 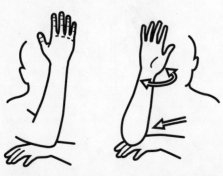 Move the elbow of your upright right arm from the back of your left wrist to the fingertips while turning the right hand back and forth.	**12. waters** 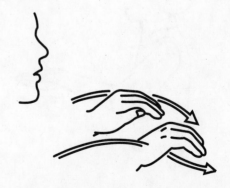 Move your hands from right to left, making the motion of waves.

This Land Is Your Land (Page 3)

13. made

With both hands in the "S" position, place your right hand on top of your left. Twist the two fists and strike them together.

14. for

Touch your forehead with your right index finger. Then point the finger forward.

15. you

Gesture ahead with your right hand, palm up.

16. me

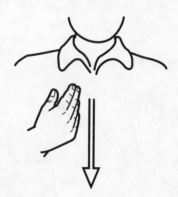

(Gesture) Move the fingertips of your bent right hand down your body.

Halloween Night (Page 1)

1. better watch out (be careful)

Hold both of your hands in the "K" position. Cross the right hand over the left, and tap the left hand with the right several times.

2. it's (is)

Touch your lips with the tip of your right index finger. Then move the hand straight ahead.

3. Halloween

Hold both hands, in the "H" position with palms in, in front of your eyes. Then move the hands apart, and turn the palms out.

4. night

Rest your right hand, in a bent position, on top of your left hand, which is held palm down, parallel to the floor.

5. look at

Hold your right hand in the "V" position, with palm facing out.

6. spooky (fear)

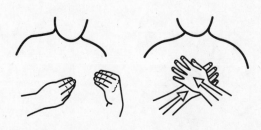

Hold both of your hands closed, with palms in. Quickly open the hands and cross them over your heart.

McGraw-Hill

Halloween Night (Page 2)

7. sights (things)

Move your open right hand, palm up, down and to the right several times.

8. skeletons

Hold both of your hands in a bent "V" position. Then cross them at your chest, and tap them on the chest several times.

9. numbers one to eight

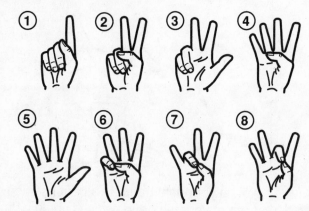

Add the numbers in sign language.

10. witches

Move your right "X" hand, palm out, from your nose to your left "X" hand, palm up.

11. goblins

(Gesture) Create your own monster.

12. ghosts

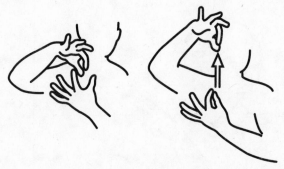

Hold your right hand above your left hand, with palms facing. Move the thumb and index finger of each hand so they almost touch and then draw apart, as if drawing out a thin substance.

McGraw-Hill

All Living Things

1. this

(Gesture) Hold your hands together, with palms up and fingers touching. Then move them apart in a sweeping gesture.

2. world

With both hands in the "W" position, circle the right hand around the left, and rest it on the left index finger.

3. is

Touch your lips with the tip of your right index finger. Then move the hand straight ahead.

4. home

Touch your lips with your closed right hand. Then move the hand to touch your right cheek.

5. living

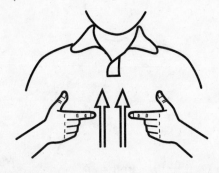

Move both of your hands, in the "L" position, up the middle of your body.

6. things

Move your open right hand, palm up, down and to the right several times. (For a bigger sign, use both hands, moving them apart.)

McGraw-Hill

SIGNING MASTER S•3•11

In the Good Old Summertime

---

1. good

Touch your lips with the fingertips of your right hand. Then move the hand down and forward, with palm up.

2. old

Grab an imaginary beard at your chin with your right hand. Then move the hand downward.

---

3. summer-

Move your right hand, in a downturned "X" position, across your forehead to show wiping the forehead on a hot day.

4. time

Point to the back of your left wrist with your right index finger.

---

5. strolling through the shady lanes (walk)

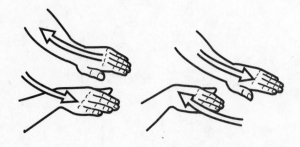

Use your hands, palms down, to show the movement of feet, one in front of the other. Move the hands in rhythm for the entire line.

6. baby (sweetheart)

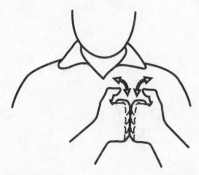

Place both hands, in the "A" position, over your heart. Then move your thumbs up and down like heads nodding.

14

McGraw-Hill

GRADE 4

		TEACHER'S EDITION page	SIGNING MASTER page

GRADE 4

Name_____

This Is My Country (Page 1)

1. this

(Gesture) Hold your hands together, with palms up and fingers touching. Then move them apart in a sweeping gesture.

2. is

Touch your lips with the tip of your right index finger. Then move the hand straight ahead.

3. my

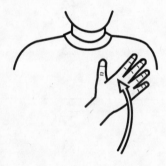

Touch your chest with your open right hand.

4. country

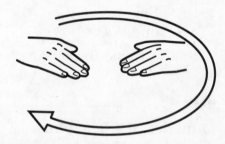

(Gesture) With both palms down and hands open, make a large circle with your right hand over your left hand.

5. land

Do the same movement you did for the word *country.*

6. birth

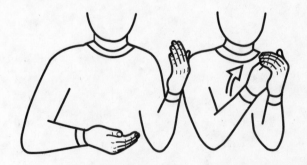

Move your right hand from your stomach into the palm of your left hand, with both palms up.

McGraw-Hill

Name_____

This Is My Country (Page 2)

---

7. grandest

Hold both of your hands up, with palms facing out, and throw the hands forward.

8. earth

Touch the thumb and middle finger of your right hand to the back of your left fist, and move the right hand back and forth.

---

9. I

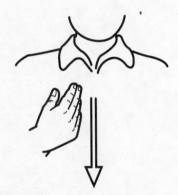

(Gesture) Move the fingertips of your bent right hand down your body.

10. pledge (promise)

Place your right index finger to your lips. Then bring your right palm to your closed left fist.

---

11. allegiance (support)

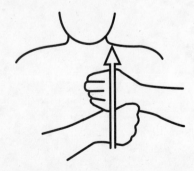

With both hands in the "S" position and your left hand resting on your right, push the left hand up with the right hand.

12. America

Interlock the fingers of both of your hands, and move the hands in a circle from right to left.

---

13. bold (strong)

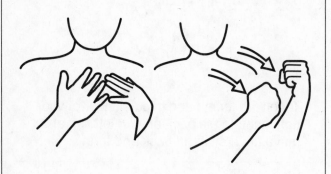

Touch your chest with your open hands, palms in and fingers spread. Then move the hands forward and into the "S" position.

14. have

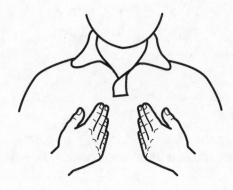

Touch your chest with the fingertips of your bent hands.

15. hold

Place both of your hands, one on top of the other, over your heart.

McGraw-Hill

Mongolian Night Song (Page 1)

1. all alone (alone)

Make a small circle in front of your body with the upright index finger of your right hand, palm in.

2. she

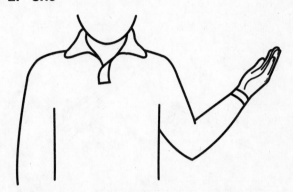

Gesture to your left side with your left hand, palm up.

3. waits

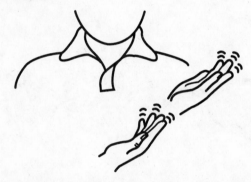

Hold both of your hands on the left side of your body, palms up, and wiggle all the fingers.

4. dark

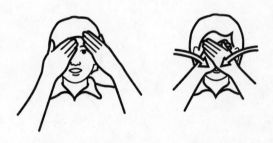

Cross your hands in front of your face, palms in, as if closing out the light.

5. I

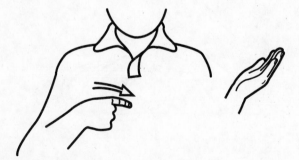

Gesture to your left with the left hand to show who is speaking. Then point to your chest with the right hand to show "I."

6. not

Cross your open hands, with palms down. Then move the hands apart (like "safe" in baseball).

McGraw-Hill

Mongolian Night Song (Page 2)

7. afraid

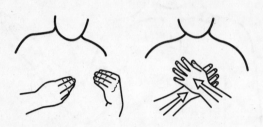

Hold both of your hands closed, with palms in. Quickly open the hands and cross them over your heart.

8. have

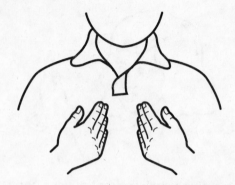

Touch your chest with the fingertips of your bent hands.

9. lamp (light)

Hold your right hand in front of your mouth, palm in, and flick the index finger off the thumb.

10. light

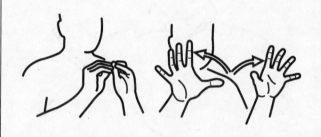

Hold both hands with palms out and fingers touching. Then move them up and to the sides, opening them to the "5" position.

11. way

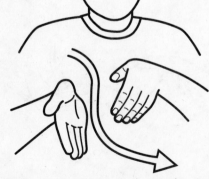

Hold your open hands facing each other, fingers pointing forward and thumbs up, and move them forward in a winding manner.

12. when

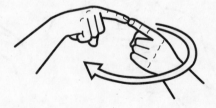

Move your right index finger around your left index finger, held palm in, and end with the tips of the two fingers touching.

Grade 4 • Use with page 19.

McGraw-Hill

Mongolian Night Song (Page 3)

13. tending (care for)

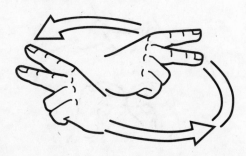

With both hands in the "V" position, rest your right hand on your left hand, and move both hands in a circle.

14. all

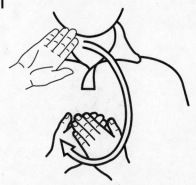

Make a circle with your right hand around your left hand, ending with the right hand in the palm of the left, with palms up.

15. think about

Make a circle at your forehead with your right index finger while showing a thoughtful expression on your face.

16. is

Touch your lips with the tip of your right index finger. Then move the hand straight ahead.

17. home

Touch your lips with your closed right hand. Then move the hand to touch your right cheek. (This is to show a place where you eat and sleep.)

One More River

1. one

Hold up your right index finger.

2. more

Hold each of your hands closed, with fingertips touching, and bring the fingertips of the two hands together.

3. river

Hold your right hand, in the "W" position, at your mouth. Then move your hands to the right, palms down, as you wiggle the fingers. Continue the sign through *river to cross.* (After the first time through, the "W" position can be dropped.)

4. numbers two to eight

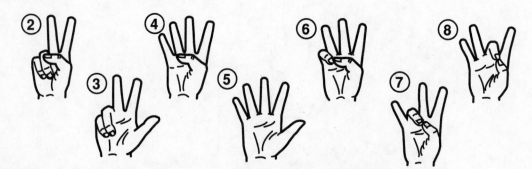

Add these numbers in sign language. For *one by one,* use left-hand "1," then right-hand "1"; and sign in the same way for *two by two,* and so on.

The Eagle

1. he (eagle)

Hold your right hand, in the "X" position, at your face to show the eagle's beak.

2. free

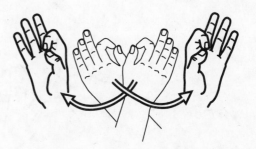

Cross your hands, in the "F" position with palms in, at the wrists. Then uncross them, move them apart, and turn palms out.

3. when (happen)

Point both index fingers away from your body, with palms facing. Then turn your hands so the palms are facing down.

4. they (people)

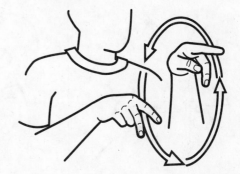

With both of your hands in the "P" position, make alternate circles in front of your body.

5. let

With palms facing each other and fingers pointing away from your body, move your hands in a scooping motion—down, then up.

6. him be (live)

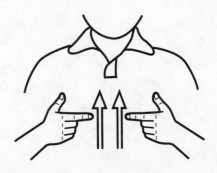

Move both of your hands, in the "L" position, up the middle of your body.

Take Time in Life

---

1. take

Hold both of your hands in the "5" position, with palms down. Then move the hands up, and close them to the "S" position.

2. time

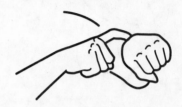

Point to the back of your left wrist with your right index finger.

---

3. life

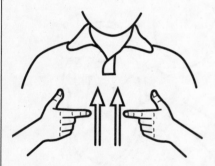

Move both of your hands, in the "L" position, up the middle of your body.

4. you

Gesture ahead with your right hand, palm up.

5. got (have)

Touch your chest with the fingertips of your bent hands. (This sign can be dropped.)

---

6. far

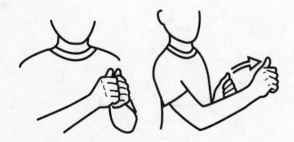

Hold both hands in the "A" position, with palms facing and fingers touching. Then move the right hand forward.

7. go

Hold both of your index fingers upright and parallel. Then move the fingers forward and down.

24

McGraw-Hill

The Cat Came Back (Page 1)

1. cat/he

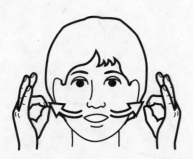

Move your hands, in the "F" position, outward from the sides of your mouth to show whiskers.

2. came back

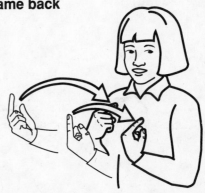

Hold up both of your index fingers, with palms in, and move them to your chest.

3. very

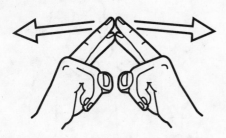

Hold both of your hands in the "V" position, with the fingertips of the two hands touching. Then pull the hands apart.

4. next

With palms in, fingers together, and your right hand closer to your body, move the right hand up and over the left.

5. day

Rest your right elbow on your left hand, palm down. Point your right index finger up, then move it in an arc to your left elbow.

6. thought

Touch your forehead with your right index finger.

The Cat Came Back (Page 2)

7. goner (dead)

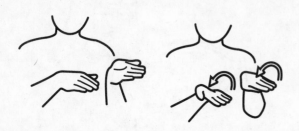

Point the fingers of both hands straight ahead, with the right palm down and the left palm up. Then turn both hands over.

8. but

Cross your index fingers, with palms out, and touch them together. Then move your hands apart.

9. wouldn't (refuse)

Move your right hand, in the "A" position with palm facing left, up and over your shoulder.

10. stay

Hold your right hand in the "Y" position, with palm down. Then move the hand down.

11. away (gone)

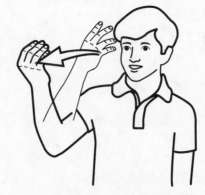

Hold your open right hand, with palm in, near your face. Then move the hand forward and away from the face while closing the fingers.

McGraw-Hill

America, the Beautiful (Page 1)

1. beautiful

Hold your right hand closed, palm in, at your chin. Then open the hand, and circle your face, coming to rest at the chin.

2. skies

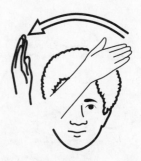

Make a large arc above your head with your right hand. Start the sign on the word *spacious.*

3. amber waves of grain

(Gesture) Point both of your hands upward, with palms facing. Then move the hands back and forth four times.

4. purple

Hold your right hand in the "P" position, and shake it slightly.

5. mountain

Strike your fists together, palms down and right fist above the left. Then raise your open hands toward your right side.

6. majesties (wonderful, great)

Hold both of your hands up, with palms facing out, and throw the hands forward.

7. above

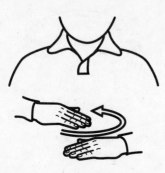

With both of your hands palms down, move the right hand in a circle above the left hand.

8. plain (land)

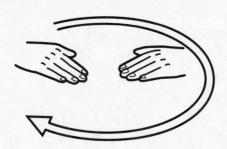

(Gesture) With both palms down and hands open, make a large circle with your right hand over your left hand.

9. America

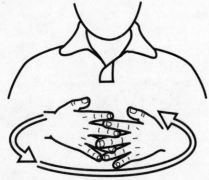

Interlock the fingers of both of your hands, and move the hands in a circle from right to left.

10. God

Raise your right hand above your head, palm facing left and fingers closed, and move it down an inch, while you look up.

11. shed (spread)

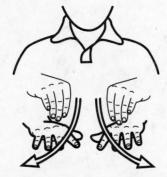

Hold both of your hands palms down, with fingertips touching. Then move the hands outward while opening your fingers wide.

12. grace (glory)

Move your middle fingers up and apart while wiggling them.

America, the Beautiful (Page 3)

13. crown (show)

Hold your left hand open, with palm facing out. Touch your right index finger to the palm. Then move both hands forward.

14. good

Touch your lips with the fingertips of your right hand. Then move the hand into the open palm of your left hand.

15. with

Hold both of your hands in the "A" position, with palms facing each other. Then bring the hands together.

16. brotherhood (cooperation)

Make connected circles with the thumb and index finger of each hand, and move your hands in a circle in front of your body.

17. sea

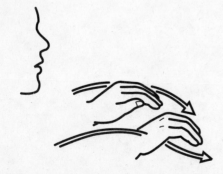

On the first *sea,* move both hands to the right, making the motion of waves. On the second *sea,* make the motion to the left.

18. shining

After the first *sea,* to the right, bring your hands back toward your face while wiggling both of your middle fingers, and get ready for the final *sea,* to the left.

McGraw-Hill

Martin's Cry (Page 1)

1. let

With palms facing each other and fingers pointing away from your body, move your hands in a scooping motion—down, then up.

2. freedom

Cross your hands, in the "F" position with palms in, at the wrists. Then uncross them, move them apart, and turn palms out.

3. ring

Hit the open palm of your left hand with your right fist. Then move your right hand out, opening and shaking it as it moves.

4. have

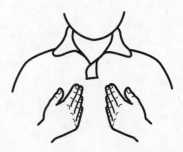

Touch your chest with the fingertips of your bent hands.

5. dream

Wiggle your right index finger as you move it away from your forehead.

6. rise

Swing your right hand down from the upward "V" position, and stand it on the palm of your left hand, which is facing up.

7. sing

(Gesture) Place your closed fingertips at the corners of your mouth. Then move your hands forward and apart.

8. all

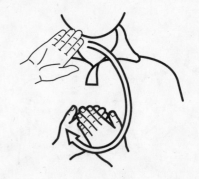

Make a circle with your right hand around your left hand, ending with the right hand in the palm of the left, with palms up.

9. men (people)

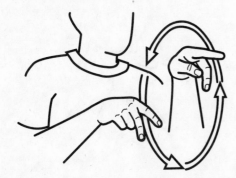

With both of your hands in the "P" position, make alternate circles in front of your body.

10. created (made)

With both hands in the "S" position, place your right hand on top of your left. Twist the two fists and strike them together.

11. equal (same)

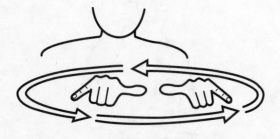

Hold both hands in the "Y" position, with palms down. Then move the hands together in a circle in front of your body.

12. black

Move your right index finger across your forehead.

13. white

Touch your chest with the fingertips of your right hand. Then move the hand in front of your face while opening the fingers.

14. red

Move your right index finger down across your lips.

15. yellow

Shake your right hand, in the "Y" position, while turning it back and forth at the wrist.

16. brown

Hold your right hand in the "B" position, and move the index finger down your cheek.

McGraw-Hill

GRADE 5

GRADE 5

1. over my head

Make a circle over your head with your right hand, palm down.

2. hear

Hold your right hand, slightly cupped, behind your ear.

3. music

Move your right hand back and forth over your left forearm. This shows the movement of the conductor's hand.

4. air (sky)

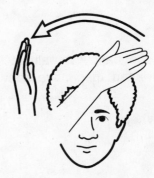

Make a large arc above your head with your right hand.

5. must

Hold your right hand in the "X" position, and move it down several times.

6. be

Touch your lips with the tip of your right index finger. Then move the hand straight ahead.

McGraw-Hill

7. God

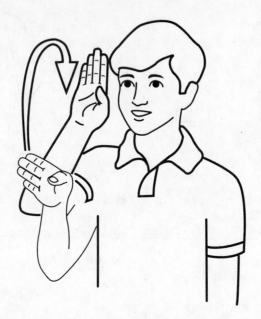

Hold your right hand with palm facing left and fingers closed. Raise the hand above your head, then move it down an inch, while you look upward.

8. somewhere

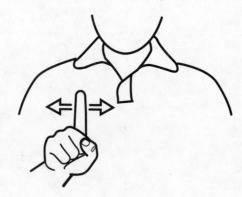

Hold up your right index finger, with the palm out, and move it back and forth.

I Got Rhythm (Page 1)

1. I

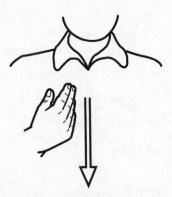

(Gesture) Move the fingertips of your bent right hand down your body.

2. got (have)

Touch your chest with the fingertips of your bent hands.

3. star-

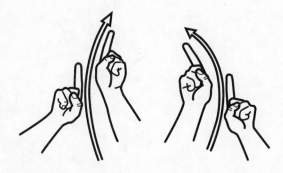

Hit the sides of your upright index fingers against each other as you move them upward.

4. light

Move your middle fingers up and apart while wiggling them.

5. sweet

Move the fingertips of your right hand down across your chin.

6. dreams

Wiggle your right index finger as you move it away from your forehead. (To extend this into a more dramatic sign, hold both hands above your head in the "C" position to form a circle, and pull them apart to make the circle larger.)

McGraw-Hill

I Got Rhythm (Page 2)

7. my

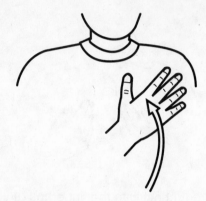

Touch your chest with your open right hand.

8. friends

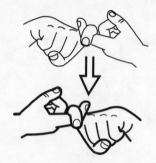

Link your index fingers, with the right hand on top. Then link them again, with the left hand on top.

9. who

Make a circle in front of your mouth with your right index finger.

10. ask

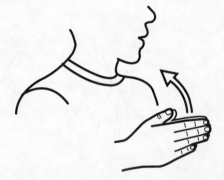

Hold your hands together, palms touching and fingers pointing away. Then turn the fingertips upward as if you were praying.

11. anything

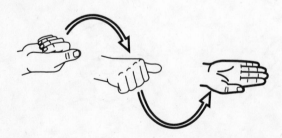

Hold your right hand in the "A" position, palm up. Turn the palm down for *any.* Then turn the palm up and open your hand for *thing.*

12. more

Hold each of your hands closed, with fingertips touching, and bring the fingertips of the two hands together.

McGraw-Hill

Everybody Rejoice

1. can you (question)

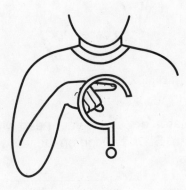

Make a question mark in the air with your right index finger toward the person you are talking to. (It is very important to show a bright, excited, and positive expression while signing this song.)

2. feel

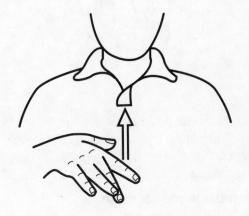

Touch your chest with the middle finger of your right hand. Then move the finger up the body slightly.

3. brand new (new)

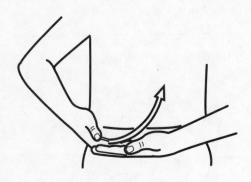

Hold both of your hands with palms up and fingertips pointing to each other. Then move your right hand in an arc across the palm of your left hand and up to the left.

4. day

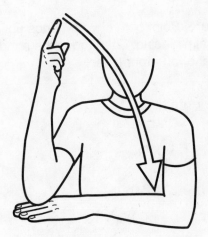

Hold your left palm down. Rest your right elbow on your left hand, and point your right index finger up. Then move your right hand in an arc to your left elbow.

SIGNING MASTER S•5•4

America, the Beautiful (Page 1)

1. beautiful

Hold your right hand closed, palm in, at your chin. Then open the hand, and circle your face, coming to rest at the chin.

2. skies

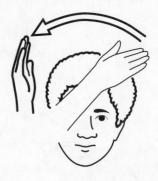

Make a large arc above your head with your right hand. Start the sign on the word *spacious*.

3. amber waves of grain

(Gesture) Point both of your hands upward, with palms facing. Then move the hands back and forth four times.

4. purple

Hold your right hand in the "P" position, and shake it slightly.

5. mountain

Strike your fists together, palms down and right fist above the left. Then raise your open hands toward your right side.

6. majesties (wonderful, great)

Hold both of your hands up, with palms facing out, and throw the hands forward.

McGraw-Hill

America, the Beautiful (Page 2)

7. above

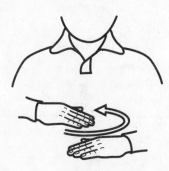

With both of your hands palms down, move the right hand in a circle above the left hand.

8. plain (land)

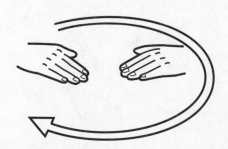

(Gesture) With both palms down and hands open, make a large circle with your right hand over your left hand.

9. America

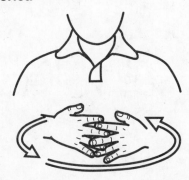

Interlock the fingers of both of your hands, and move the hands in a circle from right to left.

10. God

Raise your right hand above your head, palm facing left and fingers closed, and move it down an inch, while you look up.

11. shed (spread)

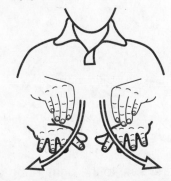

Hold both of your hands palms down, with fingertips touching. Then move the hands outward while opening your fingers wide.

12. grace (glory)

Move your middle fingers up and apart while wiggling them.

America, the Beautiful (Page 3)

13. crown (show)

Hold your left hand open, with palm facing out. Touch your right index finger to the palm. Then move both hands forward.

14. good

Touch your lips with the fingertips of your right hand. Then move the hand into the open palm of your left hand.

15. with

Hold both of your hands in the "A" position, with palms facing each other. Then bring the hands together.

16. brotherhood (cooperation)

Make connected circles with the thumb and index finger of each hand, and move your hands in a circle in front of your body.

17. sea

On the first *sea,* move your hands to the right, making the motion of waves. On the second *sea,* make the motion to the left.

18. shining

After the first *sea,* to the right, bring your hands back toward your face while wiggling both of your middle fingers, and get ready for the final *sea,* to the left.

Name_____

Swing Low, Sweet Chariot

1. swing low

With both of your hands open and palms facing up, move the hands down in a swoop.

2. sweet

Move the fingertips of your right hand down across your chin.

3. chariot

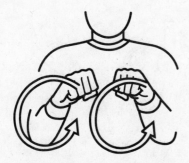

Move both hands, in the "S" position, forward in circles. (There is no real sign for *chariot*. This is a sign for *carriage*.)

4. comin'

Hold up both of your index fingers, with palms in, and move them to your chest.

5. carry me

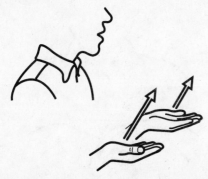

Move both open hands, palms up, upward and to the left on *me*. (Keep your left hand extended upward while you sign *home*.)

6. home

Touch your lips with your closed right hand, then touch your right cheek with the hand, as you look toward your left hand.

SIGNING MASTER S•5•6

Yellow Bird (Page 1)

---

1. yellow

Shake your right hand, in the "Y" position, while turning it back and forth at the wrist.

2. bird

Hold the back of your right hand against your lips, and use your thumb and index finger to show a beak opening and closing.

3. up high

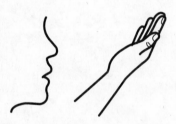

Gesture upward with your open right hand, palm facing in.

4. banana

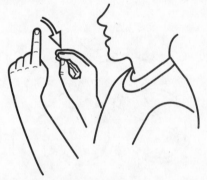

Hold your left index finger upright to show the banana. Use your right hand to show pulling down the banana peel.

5. tree

Rest the elbow of your upright right arm on the back of your left hand. Then shake your right hand, in the "5" position.

6. sit

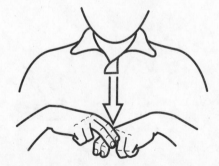

Bend both index and middle fingers slightly, palms down, and rest the right-hand fingers on the left-hand fingers.

46

7. alone

Make a small circle in front of your body with the upright index finger of your right hand, palm in.

8. like me (same)

With your right hand in the "Y" position, palm facing left, alternate between moving the thumb to the body and pointing the little finger up.

9. did (question)

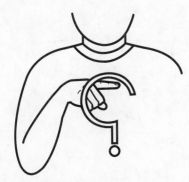

Make a question mark in the air with your right index finger.

10. lady

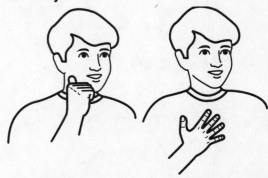

Touch your right thumb to your chin, with the hand in the "A" position, then to your chest, with the hand in the "5" position.

11. friend

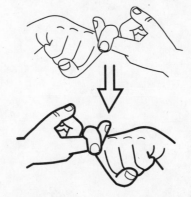

Link your index fingers, with the right hand on top. Then link them again, with the left hand on top.

SIGNING MASTER S•5•6

Yellow Bird (Page 3)

12. leave

Hold your open right hand, palm in, near your face. Then move the hand forward and away from the face while closing the fingers.

13. again

With your left hand open, palm up and fingers together, turn your bent right hand from palm up, over and into the left palm.

14. is

Touch your lips with the tip of your right index finger. Then move the hand straight ahead. Start this sign on the word *that*.

15. very

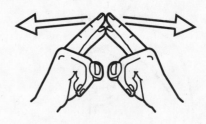

Hold both of your hands in the "V" position, with the fingertips of the two hands touching. Then pull the hands apart.

16. sad

Move both hands, palms in and fingers separated, down in front of your face, and show sadness in your face and body.

17. make

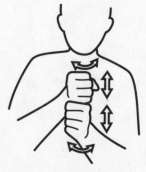

With both hands in the "S" position, place your right hand on top of your left. Twist the two fists and strike them together.

18. feel

Touch your chest with the middle finger of your right hand. Then move the finger up the body slightly.

19. bad (depressed)

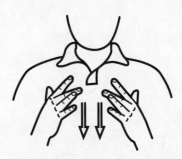

Move your middle fingers down the center of your chest. (Signs that are for unhappy feelings move *down* the body.)

20. you

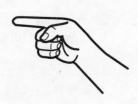

Point your right index finger to the person you are talking to.

21. fly away

Raise your open hands, palms down and right index finger against left little finger, while moving the fingers up and down.

22. sky

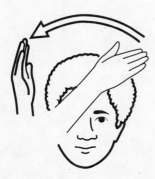

Make a large arc above your head with your right hand.

23. more

Hold each of your hands closed, with fingertips touching, and bring the fingertips of the two hands together.

24. lucky

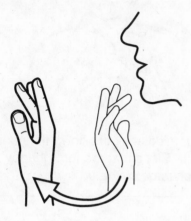

Touch your chin with the middle finger of your right hand, palm in. Then quickly move the hand away, and turn the palm out.

25. than

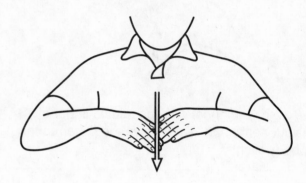

With both of your palms facing down, brush your right fingertips downward off the back of your left fingertips.

26. me

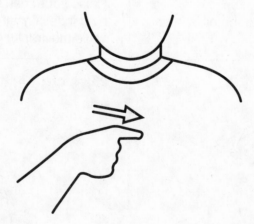

Point to your chest with your right index finger.

Name_____

1. go

Hold both of your index fingers upright and parallel. Then move the fingers forward and down.

2. my

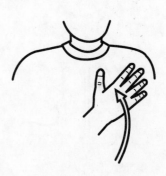

Touch your chest with your open right hand.

3. son

Touch your forehead with the closed fingers of your right hand. Then move the hand down to your left elbow.

4. work

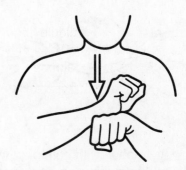

Hold both of your fists with palms facing down, and strike one against the other.

5. climb (achieve)

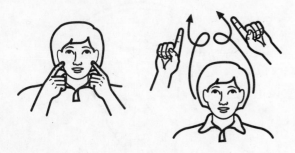

Move your index fingers from the sides of your face, forward, in a loop, and up.

6. reach

Reach your right hand up and outward, with arm straight.

McGraw-Hill

SIGNING MASTER S•5•8

Sail Away (Page 1)

1. I

(Gesture) Move the fingertips of your bent right hand down your body.

2. can

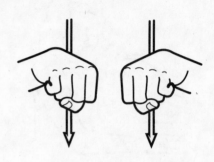

Move both of your fists downward in front of your chest.

3. hill

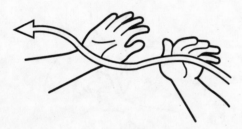

Make a wavy motion with both of your hands, palms down. Make this sign on *fly to the*, before you make the sign for *fly*, so the complete idea is easier to understand.

4. fly

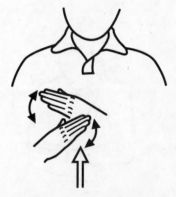

Raise your open hands, palms down and right index finger against left little finger, while moving the fingers up and down. End on *hill*.

5. reach (arrive)

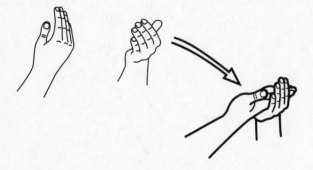

Hold both hands above your head, with palms in, and move the back of your right hand into the palm of your left hand.

6. sky

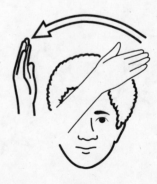

Make a large arc above your head with your right hand.

Name_____

7. but

Cross your index fingers, with palms out, and touch them together. Then move your hands apart.

8. can't

Cross your open hands, with palms down. Then move the hands apart (like "safe" in baseball).

9. separate from

Hold your index fingers upright, with palms out. Then move them apart as if they are people leaving each other.

10. friend

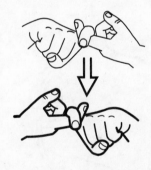

Link your index fingers, with the right hand on top. Then link them again, with the left hand on top.

11. without

Hold both hands in the "A" position, with palms facing. Touch the hands together, then move them apart and open them.

12. tear in my eye

Trace tears from your eyes down your face with your index fingers.

McGraw-Hill

For Thy Gracious Blessings (Page 1)

1. for

Touch your forehead with your right index finger. Then point the finger forward.

2. Thy

Lift your right hand upward, with palm in.

3. gracious

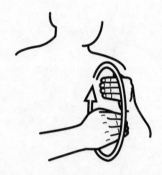

Hold both of your hands open, with palms in, and circle the hands around each other.

4. blessings

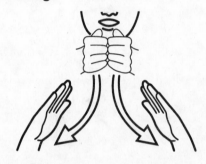

Hold your hands together, in the "A" position with palms facing, in front of your mouth. Move the hands forward, then down and out while opening them.

5. wondrous

Hold both of your hands up, with palms facing out, and throw the hands forward.

6. Word

Place your right hand, in the "G" position, on your upright left index finger.

For Thy Gracious Blessings (Page 2)

7. loving

With both of your hands in the "S" position, palms in, cross your wrists over your heart.

8. kindness

Hold your left palm open and facing up, and brush you right palm over the left.

9. we

(Gesture) Hold your hands together, with palms up and fingers touching. Then move them apart in a sweeping gesture.

10. give

Hold both hands in the flat "O" position at the chest, palms in. Move them forward and up while opening them, with palms up.

11. thanks

Move the fingertips of your right hand forward from your mouth.

12. Lord

Move your right hand, in the "L" position, from your left shoulder to the right side of your waist.

Winter Wonderland (Page 1)

1. sleigh

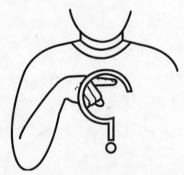

Hold both of your hands in a curved "V" position, with palms up. Move the hands back and forth together.

2. bells ring

Hit the open palm of your left hand with your right fist. Then move your right hand out, opening and shaking it as it moves.

3. are you (question)

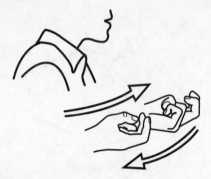

Make a question mark in the air with your right index finger toward the person you are talking to.

4. list'nin'

Hold your right hand, slightly cupped, behind your ear.

5. lane (way)

Hold your open hands facing each other, fingers pointing forward and thumbs up, and move them forward in a winding manner.

6. snow/winter wonderland

With fingers spread and palms down, move your hands downward and wiggle your fingers as they move.

Name_____

7. glist'nin'

Move your middle fingers up and apart while wiggling them.

8. beautiful

Hold your right hand closed, palm in, at your chin. Then open the hand, and circle your face, coming to rest at the chin.

9. sight

Hold your right hand in the "V" position, with palm facing out. Then move the hand from left to right.

10. happy

Pat your chest with your open hands in an upward motion.

11. to- (now)

Hold both of your hands in the "Y" position, with palms up. Then drop them down.

12. night

Rest your right hand, in a bent position, on top of your left hand, which is held palm down, parallel to the floor.

McGraw-Hill

13. walkin'

Use your hands, with palms down, to show the movement of feet, one in front of the other.

14. later

Point your open left hand upward, palm facing right. With your right hand in the "L" position, touch the thumb to the left palm. Then point the right index finger forward.

15. we'll

(Gesture) Hold your hands together, with palms up and fingers touching. Then move them apart in a sweeping gesture.

16. conspire (talk)

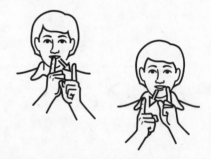

Point both of your index fingers upward, and move them alternately toward and away from your mouth.

17. dream

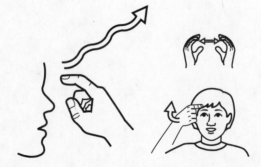

Wiggle your right index finger as you move it away from your forehead. (To extend this into a more dramatic sign, hold both hands above your head in the "C" position to form a circle, and pull them apart to make the circle larger.)

Winter Wonderland (Page 4)

18. fire

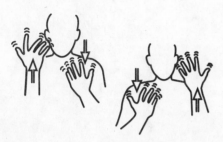

Hold both hands with palms in and fingers spread. Move the hands alternately up and down, with fingers wiggling.

19. face

Hold your left hand with palm in and fingers pointing up. Then move your right hand to face the left hand.

20. un- (not)

Cross your open hands, with palms down. Then move the hands apart (like "safe" in baseball).

21. afraid

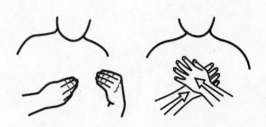

Hold both of your hands closed, with palms in. Quickly open the hands and cross them over your heart.

22. plans

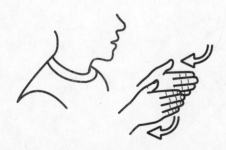

Hold both of your hands open, with palms facing each other and thumbs up. Move the hands together in arcs to the right.

23. made

With both hands in the "S" position, place your right hand on top of your left. Twist the two fists and strike them together.

SIGNING MASTER S•5•11

The Dream of Martin Luther King

1. sing about

(Gesture) Place your closed fingertips at the corners of your mouth. Then move your hands forward and apart.

2. dream

Wiggle your right index finger as you move it away from your forehead.

3. Martin (M)

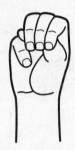

Sign the letter *M* with your right hand for "Martin."

4. Luther (L)

Sign the letter *L* with your right hand for "Luther."

5. King

Hold your right hand in the "K" position at your left shoulder. Then move the hand to the right side of your waist as if drawing a king's sash.

Evergreen, Everblue (Page 1)

1. ever- (always)

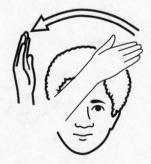

Make a circle with the upright index finger of your right hand, with palm facing in.

2. green

Hold your right hand in the "G" position, and shake it. (To make the meaning clearer, you can make the next sign, for *tree*, after signing *green*.)

3. (tree)

(Optional) Rest the elbow of your upright right arm on the back of your left hand. Then shake your right hand, in the "5" position.

4. blue

Hold your right hand in the "B" position, and shake it. (To make the meaning clearer, you can make the next sign, for *sky*, after signing *blue*.)

5. (sky)

(Optional) Make a large arc above your head with your right hand.

6. as

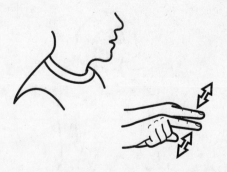

Hold your index fingers side by side, pointing forward. Move them together, apart, and together again.

7. it was in the beginning (used to)

With palms facing, fingers upright and closed, circle the open hands in turn, and move them up and over your right shoulder.

8. we've

(Gesture) Hold your hands together, with palms up and fingers touching. Then move them apart in a sweeping gesture.

9. got to (need)

Hold your right hand in the "X" position, and move it down several times.

10. see it through (succeed)

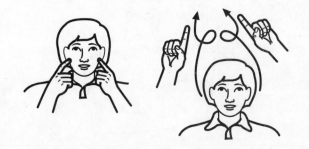

Move your index fingers from the sides of your face, forward, in a loop, and up.

11. at this point (now)

Hold both of your hands in the "Y" position, with palms up. Then drop them down.

12. time

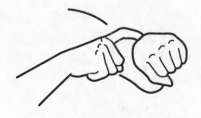

Point to the back of your left wrist with your right index finger.

McGraw-Hill

Evergreen, Everblue (Page 3)

13. up to (think)

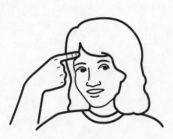

Touch your forehead with your right index finger.

14. me (myself)

Hold your right hand, in the "A" position, against your chest.

15. you (yourself)

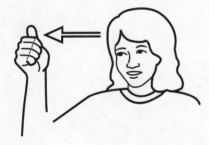

Move your right hand, in the "A" position with thumb up, toward the person you are talking to.

16. help

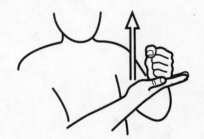

Hold your left hand in the "S" position, and push the hand up with the palm of your right hand.

17. Earth

Make a fist with your left hand, palm down. Put the thumb and middle finger of your right hand on top of the fist, and move the right hand back and forth.

GRADE 6

GRADE 6

One Moment in Time (Page 1)

1. I

(Gesture) Move the fingertips of your bent right hand down your body.

2. want

Hold both of your hands open, with palms up. Then bend the fingers and move them toward your body.

3. one

Hold up your right index finger.

4. moment

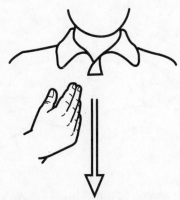

With your right index finger upright, rest the hand against your left palm. Then move the index finger forward slightly.

5. time

Move your upright right hand, in the "T" position, in a circle on the palm of your upright left hand.

6. when

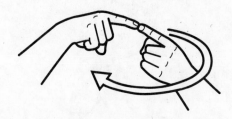

Move your right index finger around your left index finger, held palm in, and end with the tips of the two fingers touching.

One Moment in Time (Page 2)

7. more

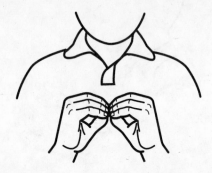

Hold each of your hands closed, with fingertips touching, and bring the fingertips of the two hands together.

8. than

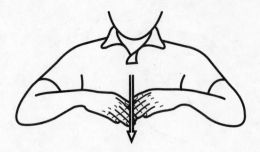

With both of your palms facing down, brush your right fingertips downward off the back of your left fingertips.

9. thought

Touch your forehead with your right index finger.

10. could

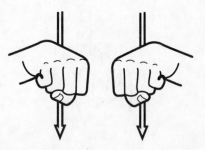

Move both of your fists downward in front of your chest.

11. be (become)

Place your right palm on your left palm. Then turn your hands so the left hand is on top.

12. all

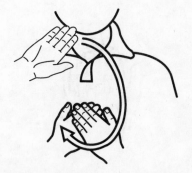

Make a circle with your right hand around your left hand, ending with the right hand in the palm of the left, with palms up.

13. dreams

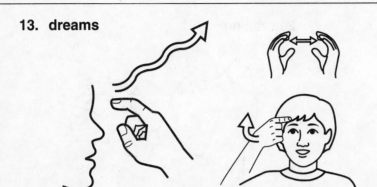

Wiggle your right index finger as you move it away from your forehead. (To extend this into a more dramatic sign, hold both hands above your head in the "C" position to form a circle, and pull them apart to make the circle larger.)

14. heart-

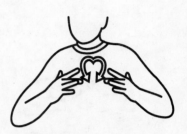

Draw the shape of a heart on your chest with your middle fingers.

15. beat

With both palms in, move your right hand back and forth between your chest and your left hand.

16. away (to goal)

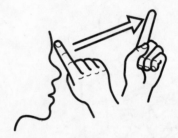

Point your left index finger upward, with palm facing right, to represent the goal. Move your right index finger from your forehead toward the left index finger to represent the person working toward the goal.

17. answers

Hold your index fingers upright, with the right near the mouth and the left ahead. Then point them forward at the same time.

18. up to me

Touch your forehead with your right index finger. Then move the hand down into the "A" position, with knuckles on the chest.

One Moment in Time (Page 4)

19. give me

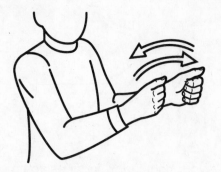

Hold both of your hands palms up, with the fingers open. Then move the hands toward your chest while closing them.

20. racing

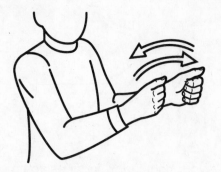

Hold both hands in the "A" position, with palms facing. Move the hands back and forth, one in front of the other.

21. with

Hold both of your hands in the "A" position, with palms facing each other. Then bring the hands together.

22. destiny (future)

Move your upright right hand, palm facing left, from the side of your face, slightly up and forward.

23. then

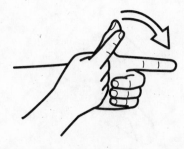

Hold your left hand in the "L" position, with index finger pointing ahead and thumb up. Touch your right index finger to the left thumb, then to the left index finger.

24. feel

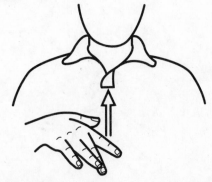

Touch your chest with the middle finger of your right hand. Then move the finger up the body slightly.

One Moment in Time (Page 5)

---

25. eternity (forever)

Make a circle with your upright right index finger, palm in. Then move the hand forward, in the "Y" position, palm out.

26. you're

(Gesture) Hold your hands together, with palms up and fingers touching. Then move them apart in a sweeping gesture.

---

27. winner

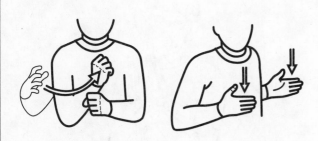

Close your right hand to the "S" position as it moves across the left, in the "S" position. Then outline a body with both hands.

28. for

Touch your forehead with your right index finger. Then point the finger forward.

---

29. lifetime

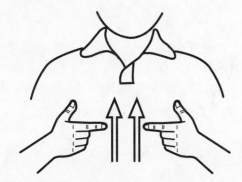

Move both of your hands, in the "L" position, up the middle of your body.

30. if

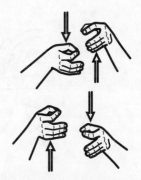

Hold both hands in the "F" position, with palms facing each other. Then move the hands alternately up and down.

One Moment in Time (Page 6)

31. seize

Make a natural grasping motion with your right hand, and change the hand to the "S" position as you turn your wrist.

32. make

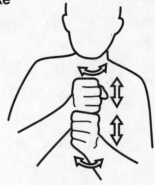

With both hands in the "S" position, place your right hand on top of your left. Twist the two fists and strike them together.

33. shine

Move your middle fingers up and apart while wiggling them.

34. be (become)

Place your right palm on your left palm. Then turn your hands so the left hand is on top.

35. free

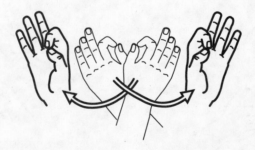

Cross your hands, in the "F" position with palms in, at the wrists. Then uncross them, move them apart, and turn palms out.

Name _____

1. harmony (brotherhood)

Make connected circles with the thumb and index finger of each hand, and move your hands in a circle in front of your body.

2. let's (let)

With palms facing each other and fingers pointing away from your body, move your hands in a scooping motion—down, then up.

3. all

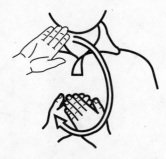

Make a circle with your right hand around your left hand, ending with the right hand in the palm of the left, with palms up.

4. join

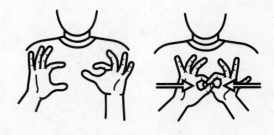

With palms out, move your open hands together, and make connected circles with the thumb and index finger of each hand.

5. sing

(Gesture) Place your closed fingertips at the corners of your mouth. Then move your hands forward and apart.

6. away (dissolve)

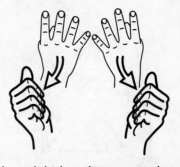

Hold both upright hands open, palms in. Then move the hands apart while touching the thumb to each fingertip of its hand. End with the hands in the "A" position.

McGraw-Hill

Harmony (Page 2)

7. hurt

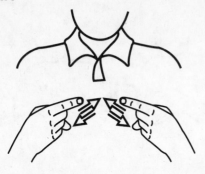

Point your index fingers toward each other, with palms in. Then jab them toward each other several times.

8. fear

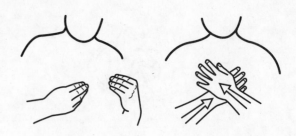

Hold both of your hands closed, with palms in. Quickly open the hands and cross them over your heart.

9. great

Hold both of your hands up, with palms facing out, and throw the hands forward.

10. new

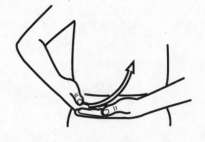

With both hands palms up and fingertips pointing to each other, move your right hand across the palm of your left hand and then up.

11. day

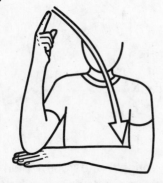

Rest your right elbow on your left hand, palm down. Point your right index finger up, then move it in an arc to your left elbow.

12. will

Move your upright right hand, palm facing left, from the side of your face, slightly up and forward.

McGraw-Hill

13. soon

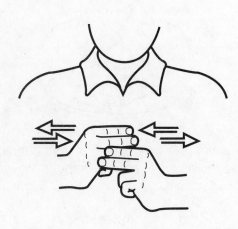

Hold both hands in the "H" position, and rub the side of the right middle finger against the side of the left index finger.

14. be

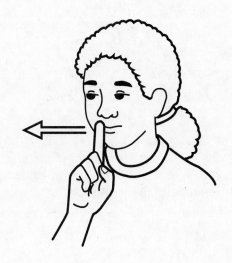

Touch your lips with the tip of your right index finger. Then move the hand straight ahead.

15. here

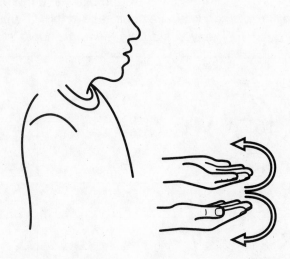

Hold both of your hands open, with palms up, and move them in small circles in opposite directions.

McGraw-Hill

American Dream (Page 1)

1. for

Touch your forehead with your right index finger. Then point the finger forward.

2. America

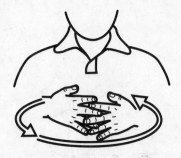

Interlock the fingers of both of your hands, and move the hands in a circle from right to left.

3. I/me

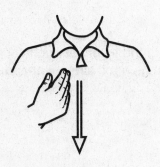

(Gesture) Move the fingertips of your bent right hand down your body.

4. dream

Wiggle your right index finger as you move it away from your forehead. (To extend this into a more dramatic sign, hold both hands above your head in the "C" position, and pull them apart.) The words *dream a dream* should be one extended sign.

5. with

Hold both of your hands in the "A" position, with palms facing each other. Then bring the hands together.

6. see

Touch your right hand, in the "V" position, to beneath your right eye. Then move the hand forward.

McGraw-Hill

7. rejoice

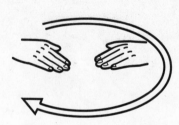

With your right hand in the "X" position, wave an imaginary flag in small circles. (Both hands can be used for this sign.)

8. yet to be (future)

Move your upright right hand, palm facing left, from the side of your face, slightly up and forward.

9. land

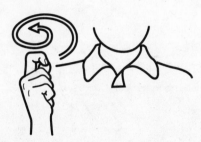

(Gesture) With both palms down and hands open, make a large circle with your right hand over your left hand.

10. hope

Point your right index finger to your forehead. Then, with your hands above your head, palms facing, bend both at the same time.

11. choice

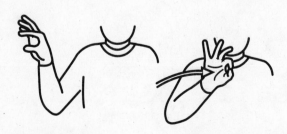

Bring your open right hand, palm facing out, to your chest while closing the thumb and index finger.

12. sea

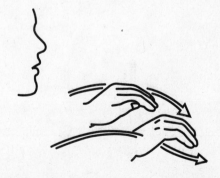

On the first *sea,* move your hands to the right, making the motion of waves. On the second *sea,* make the motion to the left.

McGraw-Hill

American Dream (Page 3)

13. shining

After the first *sea,* to the right, bring your hands back toward your face while wiggling both of your middle fingers, and get ready for the final *sea,* to the left.

14. share

Hold your left hand open, palm up, and move the little-finger side of your right hand back and forth over the left hand.

15. come/come along

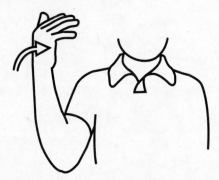

(Gesture) Make the natural gesture for *come.* Use the right hand for the first *come along* and the left for the second.

16. what

Point your right index finger, and move it down across the fingers of your left hand, close to the palm.

17. can

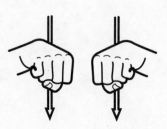

Move both of your fists downward in front of your chest.

18. be

Touch your lips with the tip of your right index finger. Then move the hand straight ahead.

McGraw-Hill

Name

1. answer

Hold your index fingers upright, with the right near the mouth and the left ahead. Then point them forward at the same time.

2. my

Touch your chest with your open right hand.

3. friend

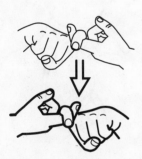

Link your index fingers, with the right hand on top. Then link them again, with the left hand on top.

4. is

Touch your lips with the tip of your right index finger. Then move the hand straight ahead.

5. blowin' in the wind

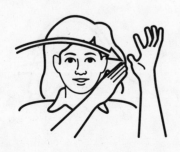 

Make sweeping gestures in the air four times with both of your hands.

McGraw-Hill

The Greatest Love of All (Page 1)

1. because

Touch your forehead with your right index finger. Then move the hand to the right and into the "A" position.

2. greatest

Hold both of your hands up, with palms facing out, and throw the hands forward.

3. love

With both of your hands in the "S" position, palms in, cross your wrists over your heart.

4. all

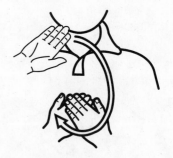

Make a circle with your right hand around your left hand, ending with the right hand in the palm of the left, with palms up.

5. is

Touch your lips with the tip of your right index finger. Then move the hand straight ahead.

6. happening

Point both index fingers away from your body, with palms facing. Then turn your hands so the palms are facing down.

McGraw-Hill

The Greatest Love of All (Page 2)

7. me/I

(Gesture) Move the fingertips of your bent right hand down your body.

8. found/find

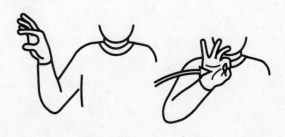

Bring your open right hand, palm facing out, to your chest while closing the thumb and index finger.

9. inside of

Hold your left hand in the "C" position, palm in and close to your chest. Then move your right hand into the left hand.

10. easy

With both of your hands palms up, brush the palm of the right hand across the back of the fingers of the left hand.

11. to achieve

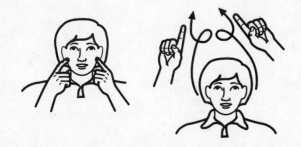

Move your index fingers from the sides of your face, forward, in a loop, and up.

12. learning

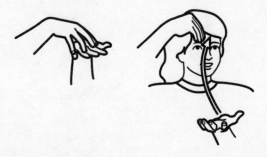

Make a grasping motion with your right hand on your left palm, and move the closed right hand to your forehead.

The Greatest Love of All (Page 3)

13. yourself

Move your right hand, in the "A" position with the thumb up, forward twice.

14. if

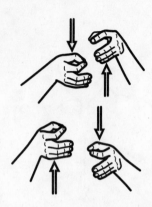

Hold both hands in the "F" position, with palms facing each other. Then move the hands alternately up and down.

15. special

With your left hand held palm in, pull up on the index finger with your right thumb and index finger.

16. place

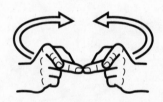

With both hands in the "P" position, touch your middle fingers together. Then separate the hands and move them in two halves of a circle toward your body.

17. you've

(Gesture) Hold your hands together, with palms up and fingers touching. Then move them apart in a sweeping gesture.

Grade 6 • Use with page 301.

McGraw-Hill

The Greatest Love of All (Page 4)

18. dreaming of

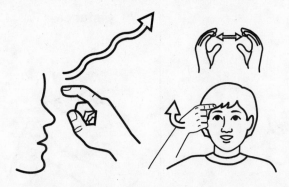

Wiggle your right index finger as you move it away from your forehead. (To extend this into a more dramatic sign, hold both hands above your head in the "C" position to form a circle, and pull them apart to make the circle larger.)

19. leads

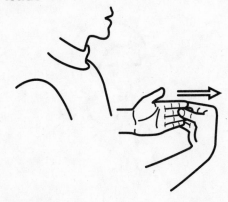

Pull your open left hand forward with your right hand.

20. lonely

Move your right index finger down across your lips and chin.

21. your

Hold your right hand with palm out and fingers together. Move the hand out toward the person being spoken to.

22. strength

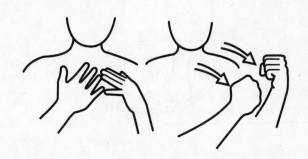

Touch your chest with your open hands, palms in and fingers spread. Then move the hands forward and into the "S" position.

From a Distance (Page 1)

1. from

Point your left index finger up. Touch your right hand, in the "X" position, to the left index finger. Then move the right hand away.

2. distance

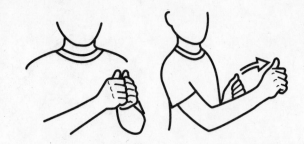

Hold both hands in the "A" position, with palms facing and fingers touching. Then move the right hand forward.

3. there/us

(Gesture) Hold your hands together, with palms up and fingers touching. Then move them apart in a sweeping gesture.

4. is/it's/they're

Touch your lips with the tip of your right index finger. Then move the hand straight ahead.

5. harmony (brotherhood)

Make connected circles with the thumb and index finger of each hand, and move your hands in a circle in front of your body.

6. echoes

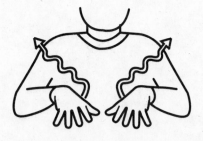

Hold your hands palms down and extended in front of your body. Shake the hands as you move them apart, upward and to the sides.

McGraw-Hill

Name_____

7. land

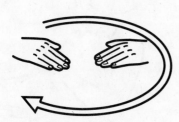

(Gesture) With both palms down and hands open, make a large circle with your right hand over your left hand.

8. voice

Move your right hand, in the "V" position with palm in, upward and forward from your throat.

9. hope

Point your right index finger to your forehead. Then, with one hand above your head and palms facing, bend both hands at the same time.

10. peace

Place your right palm on your left. Turn the hands over. Then separate them, and move them down and sideways, palms down.

11. every-

With both hands in the "A" position, draw your right thumb down your left thumb several times.

12. one (person)

Move both of your hands, in the "P" position, down in front of your body.

13. playing

Hold both of your hands in the "Y" position, and shake them several times.

14. songs

Move your right hand back and forth over your left forearm. This shows the movement of the conductor's hand.

15. God

Raise your right hand above your head, palm facing left and fingers closed, and move it down an inch, while you look up. Use alternating hands for repeats.

16. watching

On the first *watching us,* move both hands, in the "V" position with palms out, from right to left. On the second, move them from left to right. On the third, point them ahead.

17. love

With both of your hands in the "S" position, palms in, cross your wrists over your heart.

18. heart

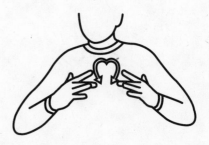

Draw the shape of a heart on your chest with your middle fingers.

McGraw-Hill

Auld Lang Syne (Page 1)

1. should (question)

Make a question mark in the air with your right index finger.

2. auld (old)

Grab an imaginary beard at your chin with your right hand. Then move the hand downward.

3. acquaintance (friends)

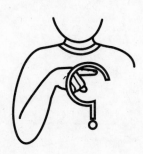

Link your index fingers, with the right hand on top. Then link them again, with the left hand on top.

4. be

Touch your lips with the tip of your right index finger. Then move the hand straight ahead.

5. forgot

Wipe your right hand across your brow, ending with the hand in the "A" position. (This represents wiping away information.)

6. never

Make a question mark in the air with your right hand, held upright with fingers together.

7. brought to mind (remember)

Hold both hands in the "A" position. Touch your right thumb to your forehead and then to the thumbnail of your left hand.

8. days

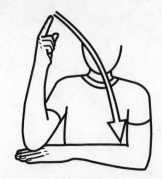

Rest your right elbow on your left hand, palm down. Point your right index finger up, then move it in an arc to your left elbow.

9. lang (pleasure)

Circle your right palm over your heart. (On the phrase *auld lang syne,* do not sign the word *auld.*)

10. syne (gone by)

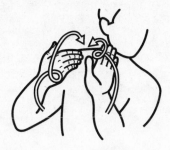

With palms facing, fingers upright and closed, circle the open hands alternately, and move them up and over your right shoulder.

11. for

Touch your forehead with your right index finger. Then point the finger forward.

12. we'll

(Gesture) Hold your hands together, with palms up and fingers touching. Then move them apart in a sweeping gesture.

McGraw-Hill

Auld Lang Syne (Page 3)

13. tak' (drink)

Bring an imaginary cup to your lips with your right hand.

14. cup (toast)

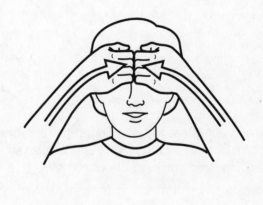

With both of your hands in the "A" position, bring them together as in making a toast.

15. kindness (nice)

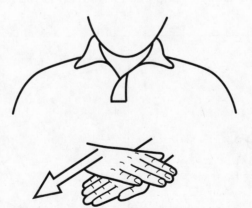

Hold your left palm open and facing up, and brush your right palm over the left.

I Have a Dream (Page 1)

1. have

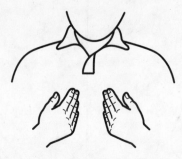

Touch your chest with the fingertips of your bent hands. (If there is a picture of Martin Luther King in your classroom, gesture toward it on the word *I*, before you sign the word *have*.)

2. dream

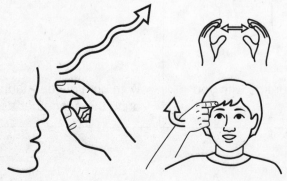

Wiggle your right index finger as you move it away from your forehead. (To extend this into a more dramatic sign, hold both hands above your head in the "C" position to form a circle, and pull them apart to make the circle larger.)

3. great

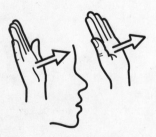

Hold both of your hands up, with palms facing out, and throw the hands forward.

4. man

Grasp the brim of an imaginary hat with your right hand. Then, with the hand in the "5" position, touch the thumb to your chest.

McGraw-Hill

I Have a Dream (Page 2)

5. used to (past)

Move your right hand, with palm in, back over your shoulder.

6. say

Hold your right index finger at your mouth, pointing left, and roll it forward in a circle.

7. words

Place your right hand, in the "G" position, on your upright left index finger.

8. would (will)

Move your upright right hand, palm facing left, from the side of your face, slightly up and forward.

9. light

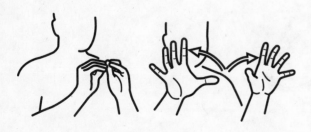

Hold both hands with palms out and fingers touching. Then move them up and to the sides, opening them to the "5" position.

10. way

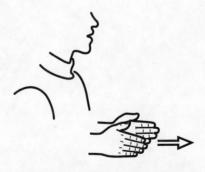

Hold both hands open and facing each other, with fingers pointing forward and thumbs up, and move the hands forward.

I Have a Dream (Page 3)

11. live

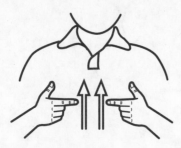

Move both of your hands, in the "L" position, up the middle of your body.

12. harmony (brotherhood)

Make connected circles with the thumb and index finger of each hand, and move your hands in a circle in front of your body.

13. all of us

(Gesture) Hold your hands together, with palms up and fingers touching. Then move them apart in a sweeping gesture.

14. are (be)

Touch your lips with the tip of your right index finger. Then move the hand straight ahead.

15. free

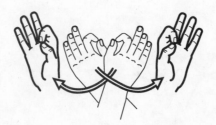

Cross your hands, in the "F" position with palms in, at the wrists. Then uncross them, move them apart, and turn palms out.

Name_____

1. many

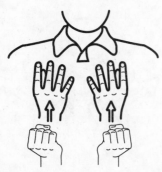

Hold both of your hands in the "S" position, with palms up, and open and close them quickly several times.

2. voices

Move your right hand, in the "V" position with palm in, upward and forward from your throat.

3. tongues (languages)

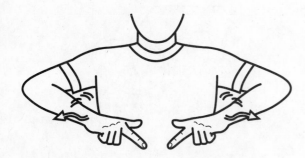

Hold both of your hands in the "L" position, with palms down, and move them apart in a twisting motion.

4. from

Point your left index finger up. Touch your right hand, in the "X" position, to the left index finger. Then move the right hand away.

5. mountains

Strike your fists together, palms down and right fist above the left. Then raise your open hands toward your right side.

6. to

Point the index finger of your right hand to the tip of the upright index finger of your left hand.

McGraw-Hill

Garden of the Earth (Page 2)

7. sea

Move your hands from right to left, making the motion of waves.

8. sing

(Gesture) Place your closed fingertips at the corners of your mouth. Then move your hands forward and apart.

9. beauty

Hold your right hand closed, palm in, at your chin. Then open the hand, and circle your face, coming to rest at the chin.

10. all around (around)

Make a circle with your right index finger around the upright closed fingers of your left hand.

11. us

(Gesture) Hold your hands together, with palms up and fingers touching. Then move them apart in a sweeping gesture.

12. in

Hold your left hand in the "C" position, palm in and close to your chest. Then move your right hand into the left hand.

Garden of the Earth (Page 3)

13. ancient (long ago)

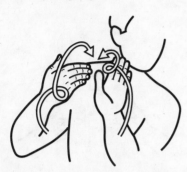

With palms facing, fingers upright and closed, circle the open hands alternately, and move them up and over your right shoulder.

14. harmony

Make connected circles with the thumb and index finger of each hand, and move your hands in a circle in front of your body.

15. for

Touch your forehead with your right index finger. Then point the finger forward.

16. glory

Move your middle fingers up and apart while wiggling them.

17. Earth

Touch the thumb and middle finger of your right hand to the back of your left fist, and move the right hand back and forth.

18. sun

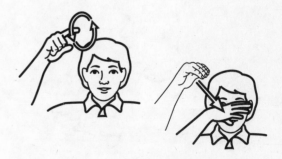

Circle your right index finger above your head. Then close the fingertips, and move the hand down while opening it.

McGraw-Hill

Garden of the Earth (Page 4)

19. sing

(Gesture) Place your closed fingertips at the corners of your mouth. Then move your hands forward and apart.

20. life/live

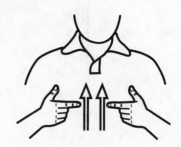

Move both of your hands, in the "L" position, up the middle of your body. Use this sign for both *life* and *live*.

21. together

Hold both of you hands in the "A" position, with palms facing each other. Then bring the hands together.

22. forever

Make a circle with your upright right index finger, palm in. Then move the hand forward, in the "Y" position, palm out.

23. as

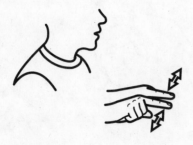

Hold your index fingers side by side, pointing forward. Move them together, apart, and together again.

24. one (united)

Make connected circles with the thumb and index finger of each hand, and move your hands in a circle in front of your body.

McGraw-Hill